What can you do to help your child?

You can help your child become a better reader and enjoy reading more by remembering to <u>EATS</u> every time he or she gets a new book. <u>EATS</u> stands for:

- **E**ncourage your children to do their reading.
- **A**sk them if they completed their tri-folds.
- **T**alk to them about the book they read.
- **S**end back the tri-folds in the mail. Postage is already paid!

We hope you have a great time reading together!

The READS Lab Team

Dear Families,

We know when children read at home — especially when families read together — student reading improves. We also understand how challenging it can be to find good reading resources and hope the books and resources we provide as part of the MORE reading program will encourage you to read!

What resources do we provide?

Over the next few weeks, you child will receive free books in the mail. Each book will come with an activity sheet called a "tri-fold." The tri-fold is a tool to help your child learn. Your child will use the tri-fold to follow the READS Reading Routine every time he or she gets a new book.

There are 7 steps in the READS Reading Routine.

1. Read the words and phrases.
2. Write your Story or Main Idea Predictions.
3. Read the book.
4. Check your Story or Main Idea Predictions.
5. Answer the questions in the student section.
6. Ask parents or other family members to fill out their part.
7. Put the completed tri-fold in a mailbox to receive prizes.

STEM CELLS

ARE

EVERYWHERE

For further information, contact:
Tumblehome, Inc.
201 Newbury St, Suite 201
Boston, MA 02116
https://tumblehomebooks.org/

Library of Congress Control Number: 2016935962
ISBN 13 978-0-9897924-9-3
ISBN 10 0-9897924-9-8

Weissman, Irving L.
Stem Cells Are Everywhere /
Irving L. Weissman, MD - 1st ed

Illustration: Barnas Monteith, Yu-Yu Chin
Cover Art: Yu-Yu Chin
Design: Yu-Yi Ling, Barnas Monteith

Printed in Taiwan

10 9 8 7 6 5

STEM CELLS
ARE
EVERYWHERE

by

Irving L. Weissman, MD

In Collaboration with

Ingrid Ibarra, PhD and Pendred E. Noyce, MD

All living things are
made of CELLS.
Frogs and fish,
birds and lilypads,
spiders and dragonflies,
are all made of CELLS.

4

Our bones, our heart,
our muscles and our brain
are all made of CELLS.

5

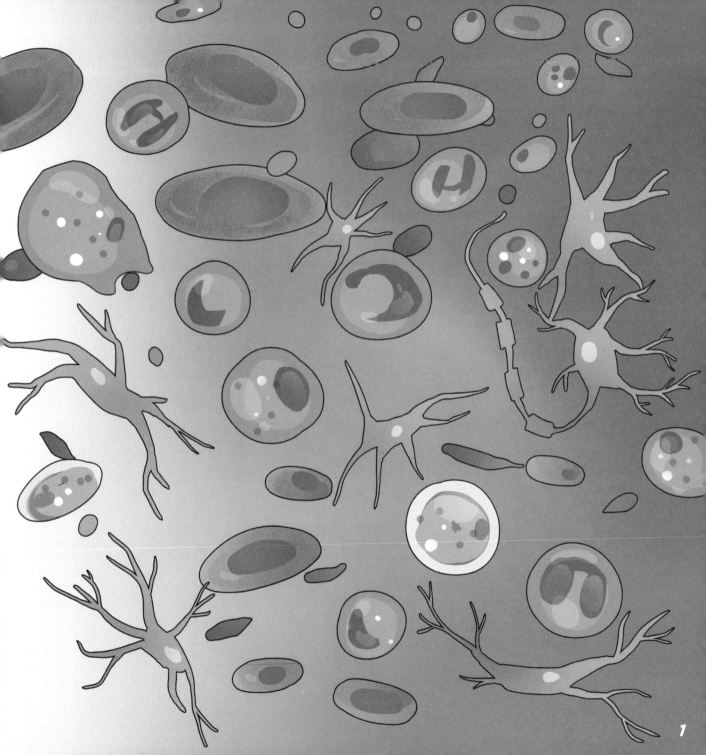

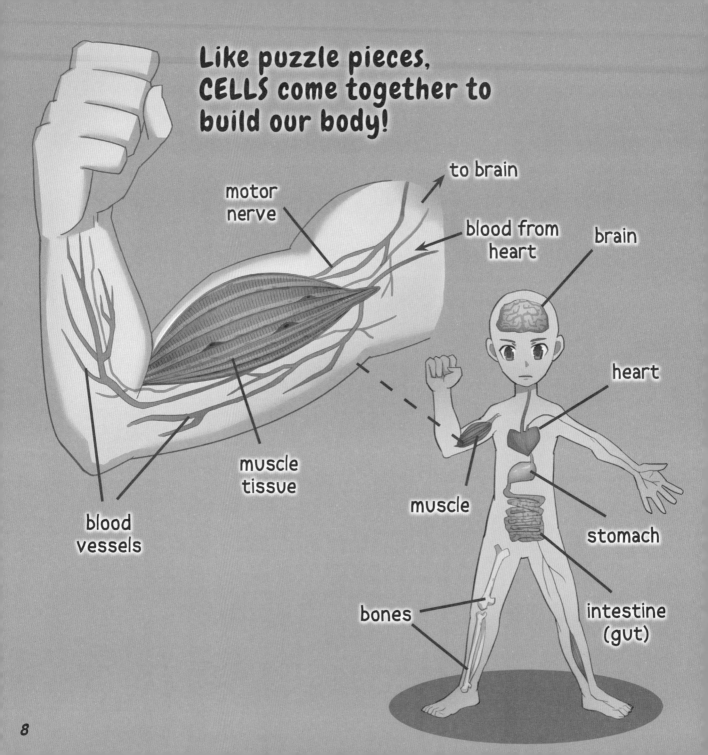

Like puzzle pieces, CELLS come together to build our body!

to brain

blood from heart

motor nerve

brain

heart

muscle tissue

muscle

blood vessels

stomach

bones

intestine (gut)

STEM CELLS!

A small group of CELLS called STEM CELLS are everywhere, in our bones, blood, muscle and skin.

They each play a special role in our body.

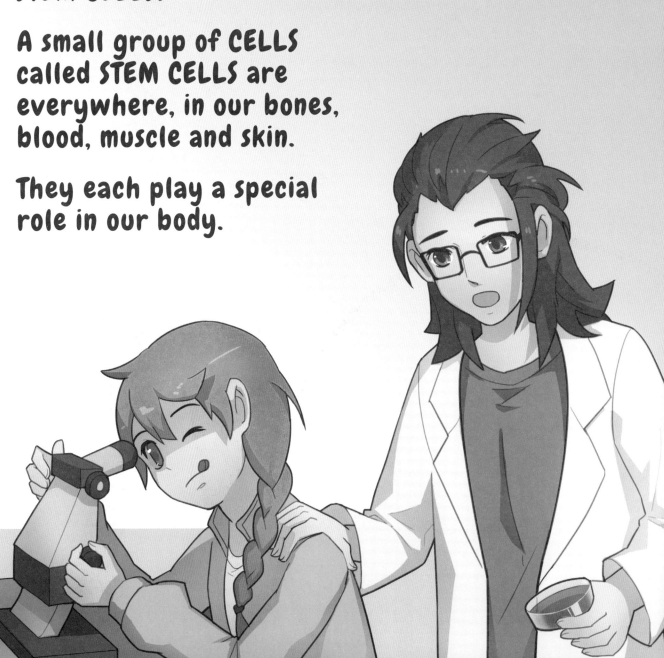

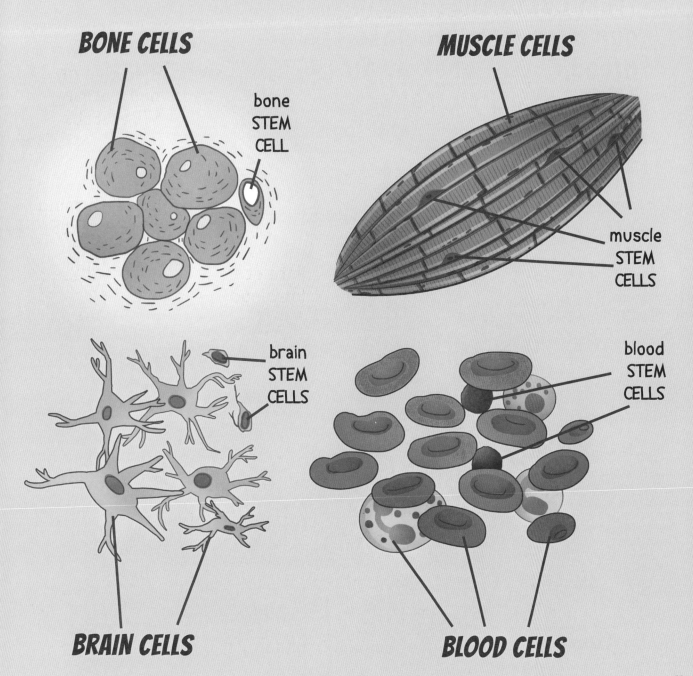

BONE CELLS

bone
STEM
CELL

MUSCLE CELLS

muscle
STEM
CELLS

brain
STEM
CELLS

blood
STEM
CELLS

BRAIN CELLS

BLOOD CELLS

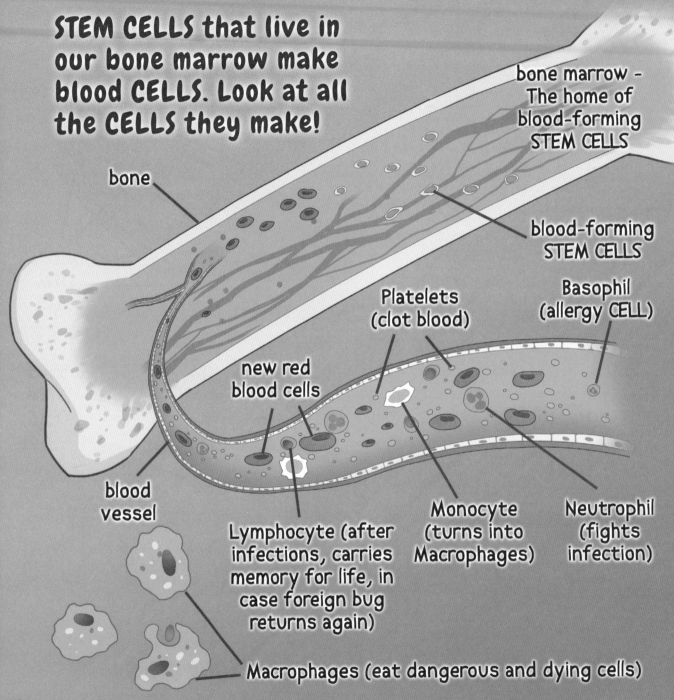

STEM CELLS that live in our bone marrow make blood CELLS. Look at all the CELLS they make!

bone marrow - The home of blood-forming STEM CELLS

bone

blood-forming STEM CELLS

Platelets (clot blood)

Basophil (allergy CELL)

new red blood cells

blood vessel

Lymphocyte (after infections, carries memory for life, in case foreign bug returns again)

Monocyte (turns into Macrophages)

Neutrophil (fights infection)

Macrophages (eat dangerous and dying cells)

We even have skeletal STEM CELLS.

These CELLS can repair a broken bone, while other STEM CELLS make the cushion in between bones (cartilage).

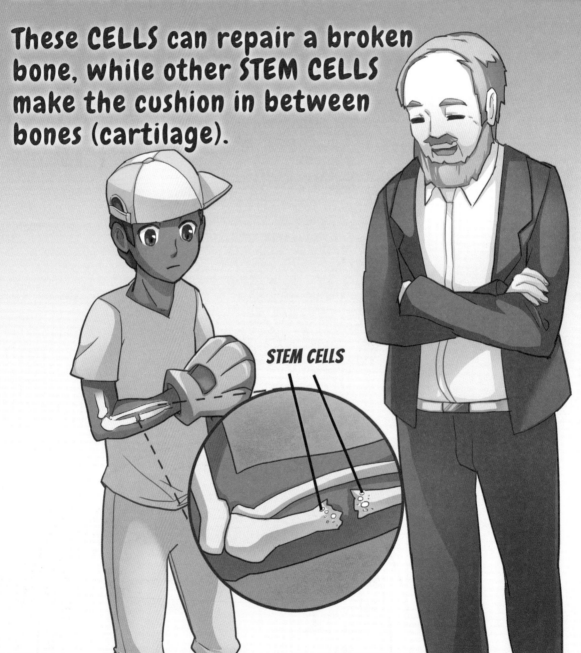

STEM CELLS

STEM CELLS
in our brain make
different kinds of
BRAIN CELLS.

These different BRAIN CELLS make connections that help us learn and think!

8 × 7 = 56

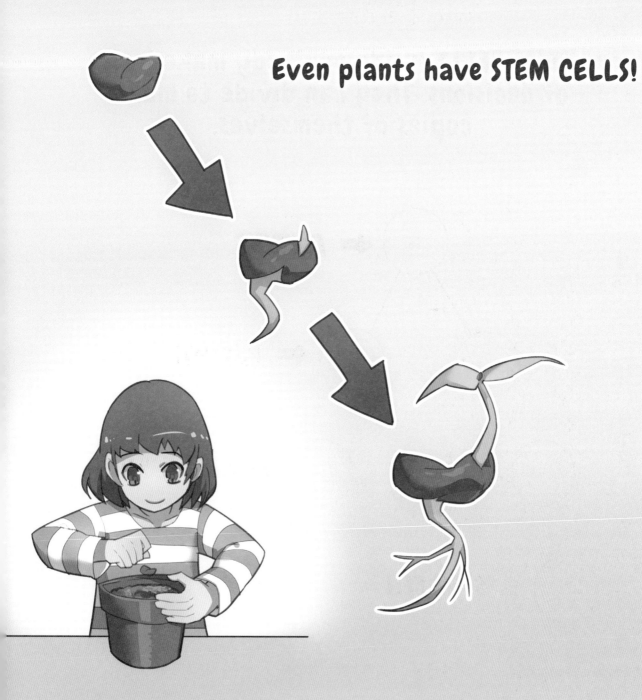

Even plants have STEM CELLS!

STEM CELLS inside our body make lots of decisions. They can divide to make copies of themselves.

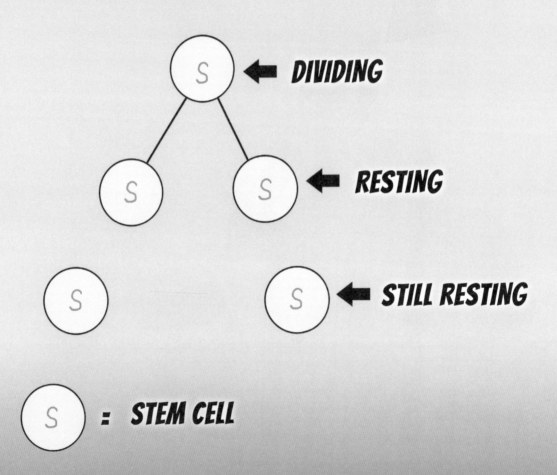

S ← DIVIDING

S   S ← RESTING

S   S ← STILL RESTING

S : STEM CELL

They can also divide to make a totally different CELL.

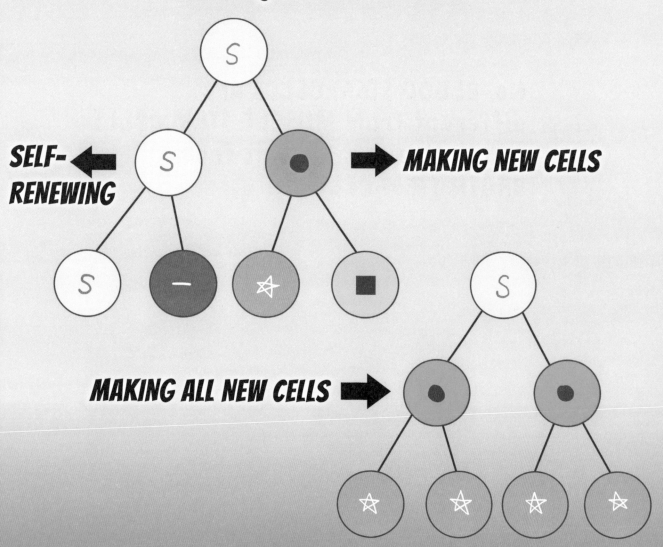

SELF-RENEWING ⬅

➡ MAKING NEW CELLS

MAKING ALL NEW CELLS ➡

Are all the STEM CELLS
in our bodies the same?

No, BLOOD STEM CELLS are
different from MUSCLE STEM CELLS
and both are different from
BRAIN STEM CELLS.

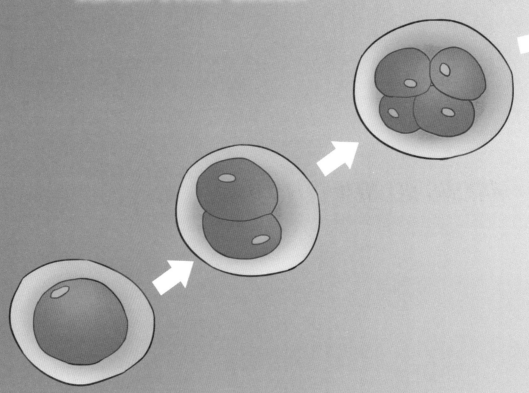

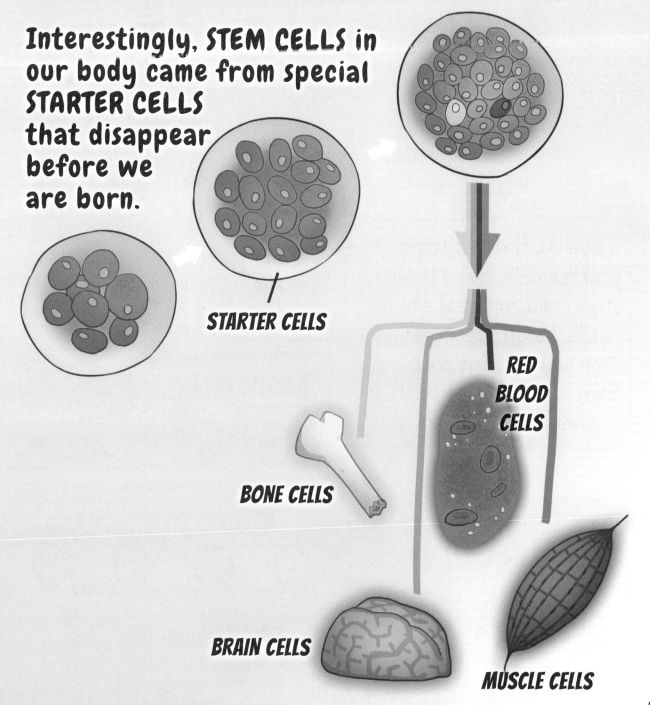

Interestingly, **STEM CELLS** in our body came from special **STARTER CELLS** that disappear before we are born.

STARTER CELLS

BONE CELLS

RED BLOOD CELLS

BRAIN CELLS

MUSCLE CELLS

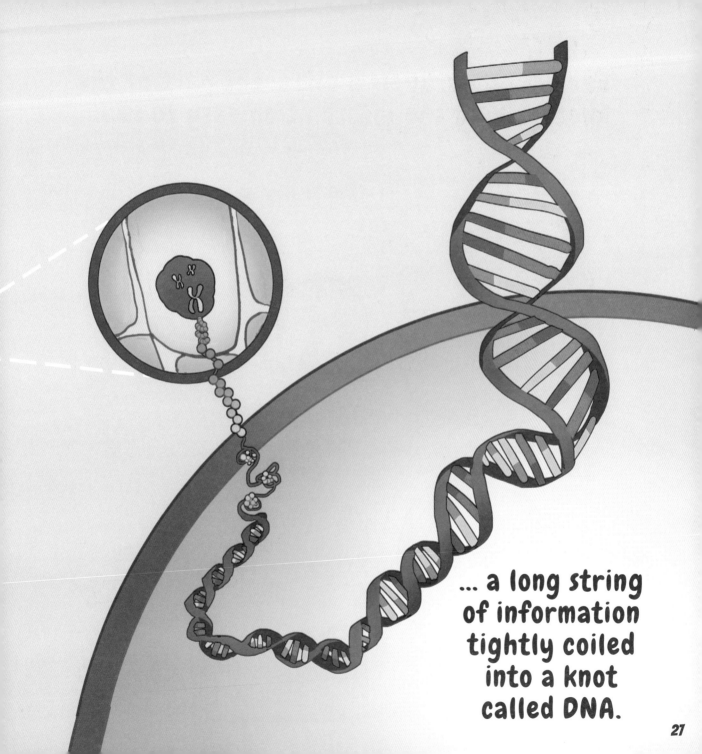

... a long string
of information
tightly coiled
into a knot
called DNA.

Each CELL unravels a different part of the knot, making the information easy to read.

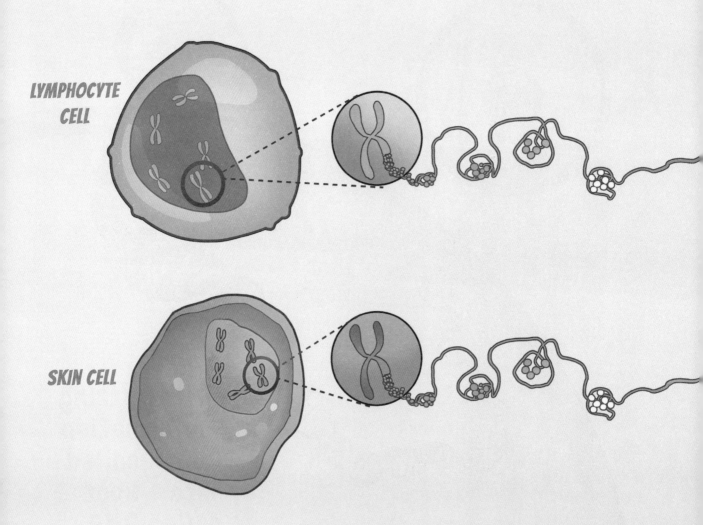

LYMPHOCYTE CELL

SKIN CELL

Blood CELLS unravel the parts with information that makes them - infection fighting CELLS.

In a skin CELL these parts remain tightly coiled.

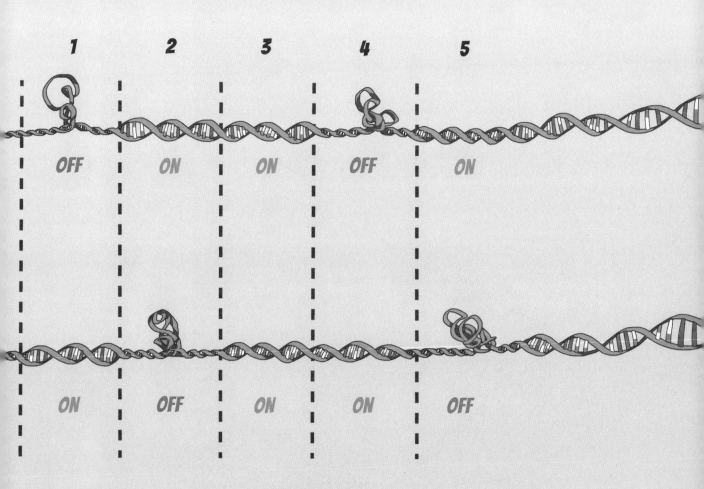

How can scientists see all the different CELLS that come from a single STEM CELL?

One way is to make CELLS glow in the dark like jellyfish CELLS.

If we color a STEM CELL green then all the CELLS it makes will be green.

Here a STEM CELL colored in blue divided and made the blue group of CELLS. A STEM CELL labeled in green made the green group of CELLS.

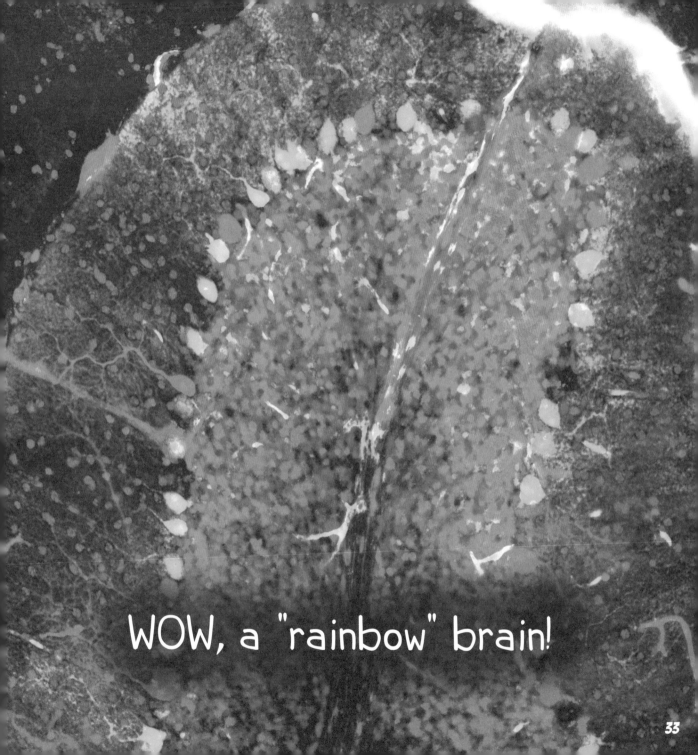

WOW, a "rainbow" brain!

The new blood STEM CELLS know just where to go, what CELLS to make and how many.

It doesn't take that many divisions to make a lot of CELLS.

Every division doubles the number of CELLS.

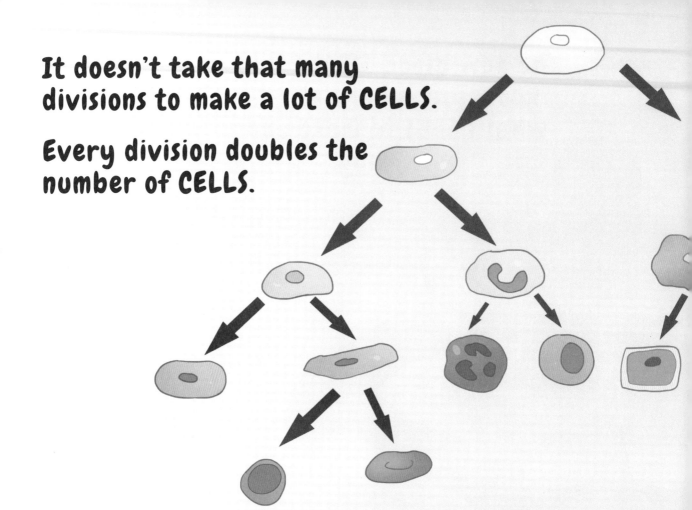

After twenty divisions, a single CELL becomes . . .

Wow! More than a million!

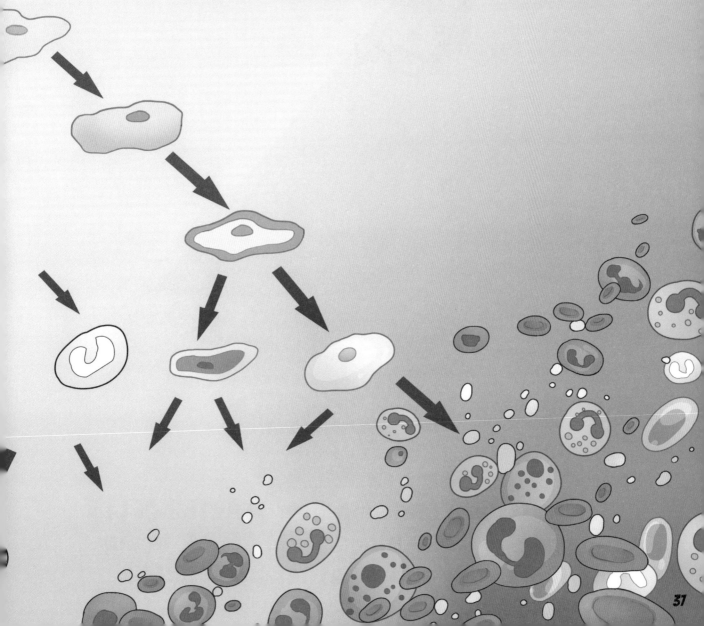

Scientists are learning how STARTER CELLS
decide to make blood STEM CELLS, brain
STEM CELLS and all other body CELLS.

If we can figure out how **STARTER CELLS** make **STEM CELLS**, maybe we can repair and regenerate **CELLS** of the body after injury.

PEDIATRIC WING

Some animals can regrow an entire body part from their STEM CELLS.

For example, deer lose their antlers every winter, and antler STEM CELLS help them regrow every spring.

An injured starfish can grow a new arm.

When a cat pounces on a lizard's tail, the tail breaks off and the lizard gets away.

Then lizard tail STEM CELLS help the lizard grow a new tail.

43

It seems that animals and plants have their own kinds of **STEM CELLS** to help them grow and even rebuild after injury. Imagine the incredible adventure **STEM CELLS** undertake to make new **CELLS**.

We can use our amazing brains to keep thinking about the world and asking questions. We can learn anything!

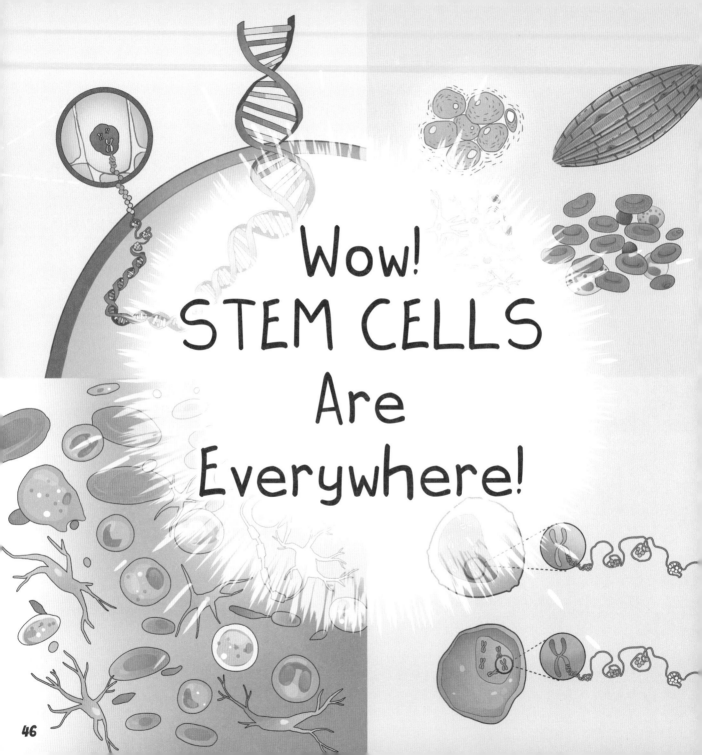

KEY TERMS & CONCEPTS

DNA - DNA is the instruction manual inside cells, arranged in long strings called chromosomes. Each cell must read its own particular part of the DNA instruction, called genes, to do its job. (pages 28-29).

Cells - Cells are the building blocks of organs (like the heart) and tissues (like the blood forming area inside bones). Each cell has a nucleus with a membrane around it. Within the nucleus are the chromosomes, containing active and silent genes. Outside the nucleus are the tiny structures that make the materials cells need or export to other parts of the body, the tiny machines that create energy for the cell, and the tiny molecules that allow cells to move from one place to another. An outer membrane separates the cells from the fluids that bathe them (pages 6-7, 8-9).

Stem Cells - Stem cells are the only cells in a tissue or organ that can divide to make one or two cells just like them (that are also stem cells). Stem cells can also divide to make different cells, starting a process called differentiation. The differentiated cells make cells that are even more different. Eventually the cells that divide and differentiate give rise to the working cells of the tissues or organs, like red cells or lymphocyte cells in the blood. Each tissue or organ has its own kind of stem cells, like blood-forming stem cells for blood, brain-forming stem cells for brain, and skin-forming stem cells for skin. Stem cells for each organ are found in that organ. Because each stem cell can give rise to many differentiated cells, only one in thousands of cells is a stem cell. Finding a stem cell in a tissue is about as hard as finding a lost needle in a stack of hay (pages 11, 20-21, 36-37).

<u>Regeneration</u> - Our bodies continually regenerate to replace old or damaged cells. Only stem cells are capable of this continual regeneration. In some animals stem cells are present at the base of the body part they make, like the lizard's tail or the deer's antlers. That way when the tail is pulled off, or the antler drops off, the entire tail or antler can be made from tail stem cells and antler stem cells (pages 40-41, 42-43).

ABOUT THE AUTHOR

Irving L. Weissman, MD is the Director of the Stanford Medicine Institute for Stem Cell Biology and Regenerative Medicine and the Virginia & D.K. Ludwig Professor for Clinical Investigation in Cancer Research Professor of Developmental Biology &, by courtesy, of Biology.

Dr. Weissman is a pioneer in stem cell research. He has authored over 800 research articles. As a high school student he performed experiments that later provided the foundation for organ transplants of all kinds. At Stanford his group isolated the blood-forming stem cells that give rise to our immune system. Purification of blood-forming stem cells suggested the possibility of regenerating tissues and replacing damaged cells with a person's own stem cells. This work set the stage for finding other tissue stem cells that scientists know today.

Irv loves to go fly fishing in his native Montana.

*All the author royalties go to support science education programs through Stanford Medicine Institute for Stem Cell Biology and Regenerative Medicine: *http://med.stanford.edu/stemcell.html*